The Liturgy of the
SOKA GAKKAI
INTERNATIONAL

Introduction

One of the most significant attributes of Nichiren Buddhism is its easily accessible practice of chanting Nam-myoho-renge-kyo. This profound yet simple method of Buddhist practice is the perfect Buddhist teaching for the modern world.

Practice is one of the three pillars of Nichiren Buddhism, the others being faith and study, through which we can bring forth our innate Buddhahood. Practice entails two aspects, practice for oneself and practice for others. Chanting Nam-myoho-renge-kyo is the primary practice for oneself. Nichiren Daishonin specified recitation of certain portions of the Lotus Sutra as a vital supporting practice for oneself. Doing both the primary and supporting practices each morning and evening gives rise to maximum joy and benefit in our lives.

Nichiren Daishonin never gave specific instructions on the format for the sutra recitation. But he did recommend reciting the "Expedient Means" (second) and "Life Span of the Thus Come One" (sixteenth) chapters of the Lotus Sutra, which are the heart of all Buddhist teachings.

He taught that our existence is identical to the universe as a whole, and the universe as a whole is identical to our existence. Each individual human life is a microcosm of the life of the universe. We recite the sutra and chant Nam-myoho-renge-kyo, the universal Law, so that our lives perfectly harmonize with the universe. Carrying out these practices activates the infinite power that the microcosm inherently possesses.

It transforms our fate, helping us to break through apparent deadlocks and convert sufferings into happiness. It creates a transformation of our inner realm, leaving us invigorated, refreshed, and positive. Through our primary and supporting practices, we develop wisdom and compassion to lead both ourselves and others to happiness.

Our twice-daily prayers establish a rhythm in our lives, moving us toward happiness and harmony. By making this consistent effort, we will attain perfect unity with the universal Law and experience the state of Buddhahood. Buddhism aims to make people free in the most profound sense; its purpose is not to restrict or constrain. Doing these daily prayers is a privilege, not an obligation. Tenacious efforts are required, but these are all for our own sake. To have great benefits or develop a profound state of life, we should exert ourselves accordingly.

As the language of the sutra is not English, people often ask if there is truly any value in reciting something we cannot understand. Certainly there is value in understanding the sutra's meaning. In addition to the translation found in the back of this booklet, there are in-depth explanations available in various SGI publications. Studying such material can help us strengthen our understanding of and commitment to the Law. But intellectual understanding without practice is of no use. Moreover, we cannot comprehend the real depth of the teachings through reason alone.

Birds have their own language, their own speech. People don't understand it, but other birds do. There are many examples among humans as well—codes, jargon, or foreign languages are well understood by experts or native speakers but unintelligible to others. Similarly, the language of the sutra is the language of the Buddhas and bodhisattvas. Whether we understand them or not, the words we chant evoke a powerful response from the universal Law, which is depicted on the Gohonzon.

Our attitude during these daily prayers has far-reaching influence. Doing the daily practice joyfully and full of high expectations brings a much more positive result than doing so grudgingly or filled with doubt.

The daily practice, especially the sutra recitation, can take some time to master. Stumbling over pronunciation is common in the beginning. Nevertheless, one's sincere attitude during the learning phase will bring the full benefit of the practice. Diligence in our Buddhist practice will enable us to savor ultimate victory.

The Silent Prayers

As mentioned above, Nichiren Daishonin never gave specific instructions on the format of our daily practice, which has changed over the centuries, all the while staying true to his intent. The SGI recommends that we recite the Lotus Sutra excerpts contained in this booklet, which are portions from the two chapters Nichiren Daishonin emphasized.

In addition, the SGI has formulated silent prayers intended to express our shared sense of gratitude and resolve as believers in Nichiren Buddhism and as SGI members. The wording of these prayers is meant as a guideline to help us express such gratitude and determination. It is not the specific wording of the silent prayers but our sincerity and heartfelt thoughts while performing the prayers that are important.

According to the principle of "three thousand realms in a single moment of life," our wholehearted prayer is powerful enough to bring forth the protective functions innate in our lives and the environment. In beginning the morning and evening recitation of the sutra, after sounding the bell and while chanting Nam-myoho-renge-kyo three times, we offer appreciation for these protective functions.

In Nichiren Buddhism, the greatest degree of gratitude is expressed through dedicating ourselves to Buddhist practice for self and others, and attaining enlightenment.

As core to the teachings of Nichiren Buddhism, the SGI regards Nichiren Daishonin as the Buddha of the Latter Day of the Law, upholds belief in the Three Great Secret Laws—which embody the fundamental Law of Nam-myoho-renge-kyo—and carries out the practice of chanting Nam-myoho-renge-kyo to the Gohonzon for oneself and for others. In several of his writings, Nichiren describes Nam-myoho-renge-kyo, the fundamental Law of the universe, as "the essence of the Lotus Sutra," which he expressed in graphic form as the Gohonzon.

Thus the first prayer expresses a vow to base one's faith on the Gohonzon and to uphold practice as taught by Nichiren Daishonin, in addition to expressing gratitude to Nikko Shonin, Nichiren's immediate successor who correctly preserved and transmitted his mentor's teachings.

The spread of Nichiren Buddhism throughout the world has been realized due to the noble efforts of the three founding presidents of the Soka Gakkai—Tsunesaburo Makiguchi, Josei Toda, and Daisaku Ikeda. To perpetuate the global spread of Nichiren's teachings and the spirit of the oneness of mentor and disciple, we honor these three presidents as the eternal mentors of kosen-rufu.

In the second silent prayer, when offering deep appreciation for the selfless dedication of the founding presidents, we are also vowing to put their guidance into practice, and to carry on and convey the spirit with which they endeavored to spread the Mystic Law.

In the third silent prayer, with the awareness that the SGI—the community of believers practicing Nichiren Buddhism throughout the world—carries out Buddhist practice as taught by Nichiren Daishonin in exact accord with the Buddha's will, we pray for the attainment of worldwide kosen-rufu and the continual advancement of the SGI.

In addition, we determine to accomplish our own human revolution, change our destiny, and fulfill all of our wishes.

Our chanting of Nam-myoho-renge-kyo and recitation of the sutra reach beyond the limits of time and space, and affect the life of the entire universe, as indicated in our prayers for the deceased and prayers for the happiness of all living beings.

These silent prayers are offered morning and evening at the conclusion of the sutra recitation and chanting of Nam-myoho-renge-kyo.

Pronunciation Guide

This book uses the Hepburn system of Romanization:

Vowels:
a	as in father
e	as in ten
i	as in machine
o	as in open
u	as in rule
ai	as in Thailand
ui	as in Louie

Consonants:
g	as in get
j	as in joy
ts	as in bets
h	as in hello
y	as in yet

Rhythm

As a general rule, there is one Chinese character for each beat, with the following exceptions:

しゃ り ほつ
舎 利 弗
shari-hotsu　　　　　　　(two beats)

は ら みつ
波 羅 蜜
hara-mitsu　　　　　　　(two beats)

Tone

Along with correct pronunciation and steady rhythm, it is also important to maintain a stable tone, neither raising nor lowering one's pitch unnecessarily.

Format

Morning and evening gongyo follow the same format:

To begin, face the Gohonzon, sound the bell, and chant Nam-myoho-renge-kyo three times (in unison if in a group). This includes appreciation to the protective functions of the universe.

Recite the excerpt from the "Expedient Means" chapter (pages 1–5). When finished, sound the bell.

Recite the verse section of the "Life Span" chapter (pages 6–17). When finished, sound the bell as you begin chanting Nam-myoho-renge-kyo.

Continue chanting for as long as you wish.

To conclude the chanting of Nam-myoho-renge-kyo, sound the bell and chant Nam-myoho-renge-kyo three times. Then offer the silent prayers (as described on pages 18–19).

妙法蓮華經。
Myō hō ren ge kyō.

方便品。第二。
Hōben-pon. Dai ni.

爾時世尊。從三昧。安詳
Niji seson. Jū sanmai. Anjō

而起。告舍利弗。諸
ni ki. Gō shari-hotsu. Sho-

佛智慧。甚深無量。其
but chi-e. Jinjin muryō. Go

智慧門。難解難入。一切
chi-e mon. Nange nannyū. Issai

聲聞。辟支佛。所
shōmon. Hyaku-shi-butsu. Sho

不能知。所以者何。佛
fu nō chi. Sho-i sha ga. Butsu

曾親近。百千萬億。
zō shingon. Hyaku sen man noku.

1

無数諸佛。盡行
Mushu sho butsu. Jin gyō

諸佛。無量道法。勇猛
sho-butsu. Muryō dōhō. Yūmyō

精進。名稱普聞。成就
shōjin. Myōshō fu mon. Jōju

甚深。未曾有法。隨宜所
jinjin. Mi-zō-u hō. Zui gi sho

說。意趣難解。舍利弗。
setsu. Ishu nange. Shari-hotsu.

吾從成佛已來。種種因緣。
Go jū jō-butsu irai. Shuju innen.

種種譬喩。廣演言教。無
Shuju hiyu. Kō en gonkyō. Mu

數方便。引導衆生。令離
shu hōben. Indō shujō. Ryō ri

諸著。所以者何。如來
sho jaku. Sho-i sha ga. Nyorai

2

方便。知見波羅蜜。皆
hōben. Chi-ken hara-mitsu. Kai

已具足。舍利弗。如來
i gu-soku. Shari-hotsu. Nyorai

知見。廣大深遠。無量
chi-ken. Kōdai jinnon. Muryō

無礙。力。無所畏。禪定。
muge. Riki. Mu-sho-i. Zenjō.

解脱。三昧。深入無際。
Gedas. Sanmai. Jin nyū musai.

成就一切。未曾有法。舍利
Jōju issai. Mi-zō-u hō. Shari-

弗。如來能。種種分
hotsu. Nyorai nō. Shuju fun-

別。巧説諸法。言
betsu. Gyō ses sho hō. Gon-

辭柔軟。悦可衆心。舍利
ji nyūnan. Ekka shushin. Shari-

弗。 取要言之。無量
hotsu. Shu yō gon shi. Muryō

無邊。未曾有法。佛悉
muhen. Mi-zō-u hō. Bus͡shitsu

成就。止舍利弗。不須復
jōju. Shi shari-hotsu. Fu shu bu

說。所以者何。佛所
setsu. Sho-i sha ga. Bus͡sho

成就。第一希有。難解之
jōju. Dai ichi ke-u. Nange shi

法。唯佛與佛。乃能
hō. Yui butsu yo butsu. Nai nō

究盡。諸法實相。
kujin. Shohō jissō.

所謂諸法。如是相。
Sho-i shohō. Nyo ze sō.

如是性。如是體。
Nyo ze shō. Nyo ze tai.

如 是 力。 如 是 作。

Nyo ze riki. Nyo ze sa.

如 是 因。 如 是 縁。

Nyo ze in. Nyo ze en.

如 是 果。 如 是 報。

Nyo ze ka. Nyo ze hō.

如 是 本 末 究 竟 等。

Nyo ze honmak kukyō tō.

(Recite the section from ″Sho-i shohō″ to ″Nyo ze honmak kukyō tō″ three times.)

5

妙　法蓮華經。
Myō hō ren ge kyō.

如　來壽量品。第十六。
Nyorai ju-ryō-hon. Dai jū-roku.

自我得佛來。
Ji ga toku bur͡rai.

所　經　諸　劫數。
Sho kyō sho kosshu.

無　量　百　千　萬。
Muryō hyaku sen man.

億　載　阿僧祇。
Oku sai asōgi.

常說法教化。
Jō seppō kyōke.

無　數　億衆生。
Mushu oku shujō.

令　入於佛道。
Ryō nyū o butsu-dō.

6

爾來無量劫。
Nirai muryō kō.

爲度衆生故。
I do shujō ko.

方便現涅槃。
Hōben gen nehan.

而實不滅度。
Ni jitsu fu metsu-do.

常住此說法。
Jō jū shi seppō.

我常住於此。
Ga jō jū o shi.

以諸神通力。
I sho jin-zū-riki.

令顚倒衆生。
Ryō tendō shujō.

雖近而不見。
Sui gon ni fu ken.

衆　見我滅　度。
Shu ken ga metsu-do.

廣　供養舍利。
Kō kuyō shari.

咸　皆懷戀慕。
Gen kai e renbo.

而生　渇　仰心。
Ni shō katsu-gō shin.

衆　生既信　伏。
Shujō ki shin-buku.

質　　直意柔　頓。
Shichi-jiki i nyūnan.

一心欲見　佛。
Isshin yok ken butsu.

不自惜　身命。
Fu ji shaku shinmyō.

時我及　衆僧。
Ji ga gyū shusō.

倶　出　靈鷲山。
Ku shutsu ryōjusen.

我　時　語　衆　生。
Ga ji go shujō.

常　在　此　不　滅。
Jō zai shi fu-metsu.

以方　便　力　故。
I hō-ben-rik ko.

現　有　滅　不　滅。
Gen u metsu fu-metsu.

餘　國　有　衆　生。
Yo-koku u shujō.

恭　敬　信　樂　者。
Kugyō shingyō sha.

我　復於彼　中。
Ga bu o hi chū.

爲　說　無上法。
I setsu mujō hō.

汝 等 不 聞 此。
Nyotō fu mon shi.

但 謂 我 滅 度。
Tan ni ga metsu-do.

我 見 諸 衆 生。
Ga ken sho shujō.

沒 在 於 苦 海。
Motsu-zai o kukai.

故 不 爲 現 身。
Ko fu i gen shin.

令 其 生 渴 仰。
Ryō go shō katsu-gō.

因 其 心 戀 慕。
In go shin renbo.

乃 出 爲 説 法。
Nai shutsu i seppō.

神 通 力 如 是。
Jin-zū-riki nyo ze.

於 阿 僧 祇 劫。
（お あ そうぎ こう）

O asōgi kō.

常 在 靈 鷲 山。
（じょう ざい りょうじゅ せん）

Jō zai ryōjusen.

及 餘 諸 住 處。
（ぎゅう よ しょ じゅう しょ）

Gyū yo sho jūsho.

衆 生 見 劫 盡。
（しゅ じょう けん こう じん）

Shujō ken kō jin.

大 火 所 燒 時。
（だい か しょ しょう じ）

Dai ka sho shō ji.

我 此 土 安 穩。
（が し ど あん のん）

Ga shi do annon.

天 人 常 充 滿。
（てん にん じょう じゅう まん）

Tennin jō jūman.

園 林 諸 堂 閣。
（おん りん しょ どう かく）

Onrin sho dō-kaku.

種 種 寶 莊 嚴。
（しゅ じゅ ほう しょう ごん）

Shuju hō shōgon.

11

寶樹多華果。
Hōju ta keka.

衆生所遊樂。
Shujō sho yū-raku.

諸天擊天皷。
Shoten gyaku tenku.

常作衆伎樂。
Jō sas͡shu gi-gaku.

雨曼佗羅華。
U mandara ke.

散佛及大衆。
San butsu gyū daishu.

我淨土不毀。
Ga jōdo fu ki.

而衆見燒盡。
Ni shu ken shō jin.

憂怖諸苦惱。
Ufu sho kunō.

如是悉充滿。
Nyo ze shitsu jūman.

是諸罪衆生。
Ze sho zai shujō.

以惡業因縁。
I aku-gō innen.

過 阿僧祇劫。
Ka asōgi kō.

不聞三寶名。
Fu mon sanbō myō.

諸有修功德。
Sho u shu ku-doku.

柔和質直者。
Nyūwa shichi-jiki sha.

則皆見我身。
Sokkai ken gashin.

在此而説法。
Zai shi ni seppō.

或時爲此衆。
Waku-ji i shi shu.

說佛壽無量。
Setsu butsu-ju muryō.

久乃見佛者。
Ku nai ken bussha.

爲說佛難値。
I setsu butsu nan chi.

我智力如是。
Ga chi-riki nyo ze.

慧光照無量。
Ekō shō muryō.

壽命無數劫。
Jumyō mushu kō.

久修業所得。
Ku shugō sho toku.

汝等有智者。
Nyotō u chi sha.

14

勿於此生疑。
Mot̂ to shi shō gi.

當斷令永盡。
Tō dan ryō yō jin.

佛語實不虛。
Butsu-go jip̂ puko.

如醫善方便。
Nyo i zen hōben.

爲治狂子故。
I ji ō shi ko.

實在而言死。
Jitsu zai ni gon shi.

無能說虛妄。
Mu nō sek̂ komō.

我亦爲世父。
Ga yaku i se bu.

救諸苦患者。
Ku sho kugen sha.

爲凡夫顛倒。
I bonbu tendō.

實在而言滅。
Jitsu zai ni gon metsu.

以常見我故。
I jōken ga ko.

而生憍恣心。
Ni shō kyōshi shin.

放逸著五欲。
Hō-itsu jaku go-yoku.

墮於惡道中。
Da o aku-dō chū.

我常知衆生。
Ga jō chi shujō.

行道不行道。
Gyō dō fu gyō dō.

隨應所可度。
Zui ō sho ka do.

爲說　種種法。
I ses͡shuju hō.

毎　自作是　念。
Mai ji sa ze nen.

以何　令　衆生。
I ga ryō shujō.

得　　入　無　上　道。
Toku nyū mu-jō dō.

速　成就佛　身。
Soku jōju busshin.

17

Appreciation to the Gohonzon

I offer my profound gratitude and appreciation to the Gohonzon, which embodies Nam-myoho-renge-kyo, the essence of the Lotus Sutra.

I offer my profound gratitude and appreciation to Nichiren Daishonin, the Buddha of the Latter Day of the Law.

I offer my profound gratitude and appreciation to Nikko Shonin.

Chant Nam-myoho-renge-kyo three times.

Appreciation for the Three Founding Presidents

I offer my deepest appreciation for the three founding presidents of the Soka Gakkai—Tsunesaburo Makiguchi, Josei Toda, and Daisaku Ikeda—the eternal mentors of kosen-rufu, for their selfless dedication to propagating the Law.

Chant Nam-myoho-renge-kyo three times.

Prayers for Worldwide Kosen-rufu and for the Deceased

I pray that the great vow for worldwide kosen-rufu be fulfilled and that the Soka Gakkai International will develop in this endeavor for countless generations to come.

I pray to accomplish my own human revolution, change my destiny, and fulfill all of my wishes. (*Offer additional prayers here.*)

I pray for my deceased relatives, fellow members, friends, and all those who have passed away, particularly for these individuals: (*Sound the bell continuously while offering prayers.*)

Chant Nam-myoho-renge-kyo three times.

I pray for peace throughout the world and the happiness of all living beings.

Sound the bell and chant Nam-myoho-renge-kyo three times to conclude (if in a group, chant in unison).

Excerpts from the Lotus Sutra
Chapter 2: Expedient Means

At that time the world-honored one calmly arose from his samadhi and addressed Shariputra, saying: "The wisdom of the Buddhas is infinitely profound and immeasurable. The door to this wisdom is difficult to understand and difficult to enter. Not one of the voice-hearers or pratyekabuddhas is able to comprehend it.

"What is the reason for this? The Buddhas have personally attended a hundred, a thousand, ten thousand, a million, a countless number of Buddhas and have fully carried out an immeasurable number of Buddhas' ways and doctrines. They have exerted themselves bravely and vigorously, and their names are universally known. They have realized the Law that is profound and never known before, and preach it in accordance with what is appropriate, yet their intentions are difficult to understand.

"Shariputra, ever since I attained Buddhahood I have through various causes and various similes widely expounded my teachings and have used countless expedient means to guide living beings and cause them to renounce their attachments. Why is this? Because the thus come ones are fully possessed of both expedient means and the paramita of wisdom.

"Shariputra, the wisdom of the thus come ones is expansive and profound. They have immeasurable [compassion], unlimited [eloquence], power, fearlessness, concentration, emancipation, and samadhis, and have deeply entered the boundless and awakened to the Law never before attained.

"Shariputra, the thus come ones know how to make various distinctions and to expound the teachings skillfully. Their words are soft and gentle and can delight the hearts of the assembly.

"Shariputra, to sum it up: the Buddhas have fully realized the Law that is limitless, boundless, never attained before.

"But stop, Shariputra, I will say no more. Why? Because what the Buddhas have achieved is the rarest and most difficult-to-understand Law. The true aspect of all phenomena can only be understood and shared between Buddhas. This reality consists of the appearance, nature, entity, power, influence, internal cause, relation, latent effect, manifest effect, and their consistency from beginning to end." (*The Lotus Sutra and Its Opening and Closing Sutras,* pp. 56–57)

Chapter 16: The Life Span of the Thus Come One

Since I attained Buddhahood
the number of kalpas that have passed
is an immeasurable hundreds, thousands,
    ten thousands,
millions, trillions, asamkhyas.
Constantly I have preached the Law, teaching,
    converting
countless millions of living beings,
causing them to enter the Buddha way,
all this for immeasurable kalpas.
In order to save living beings,

as an expedient means I appear to enter nirvana
but in truth I do not pass into extinction.
I am always here, preaching the Law.
I am always here,
but through my transcendental powers
I make it so that living beings in their befuddlement
do not see me even when close by.
When the multitude sees that I have passed into
    extinction,
far and wide they offer alms to my relics.
All harbor thoughts of yearning
and in their minds thirst to gaze at me.
When living beings have become truly faithful,
honest and upright, gentle in intent,
single-mindedly desiring to see the Buddha,
not hesitating even if it costs them their lives,
then I and the assembly of monks
appear together on Holy Eagle Peak.
At that time I tell the living beings
that I am always here, never entering extinction,
but that because of the power of expedient means
at times I appear to be extinct, at other times not,
and that if there are living beings in other lands
who are reverent and sincere in their wish
    to believe,
then among them too
I will preach the unsurpassed Law.
But you have not heard of this,
so you suppose that I enter extinction.
When I look at living beings
I see them drowned in a sea of suffering;
therefore I do not show myself,

causing them to thirst for me.
Then when their minds are filled with yearning,
at last I appear and preach the Law for them.
Such are my transcendental powers.
For asamkhya kalpas
constantly I have dwelled on Holy Eagle Peak
and in various other places.
When living beings witness the end of a kalpa
and all is consumed in a great fire,
this, my land, remains safe and tranquil,
constantly filled with heavenly and human beings.
The halls and pavilions in its gardens and groves
are adorned with various kinds of gems.
Jeweled trees abound in flowers and fruit
where living beings enjoy themselves at ease.
The gods strike heavenly drums,
constantly making many kinds of music.
Mandarava blossoms rain down,
scattering over the Buddha and the great
    assembly.
My pure land is not destroyed,
yet the multitude sees it as consumed in fire,
with anxiety, fear and other sufferings
filling it everywhere.
These living beings with their various offenses,
through causes arising from their evil actions,
spend asamkhya kalpas
without hearing the name of the three treasures.
But those who practice meritorious ways,
who are gentle, peaceful, honest, and upright,
all of them will see me
here in person, preaching the Law.

At times for this multitude
I describe the Buddha's life span as immeasurable,
and to those who see the Buddha only after
    a long time
I explain how difficult it is to meet a Buddha.
Such is the power of my wisdom
that its sagacious beams shine without measure.
This life span of countless kalpas
I gained as the result of lengthy practice.
You who are possessed of wisdom,
entertain no doubts on this point!
Cast them off, end them forever,
for the Buddha's words are true, not false.
He is like a skilled physician
who uses an expedient means to cure
    his deranged sons.
Though in fact alive, he gives out word he is dead,
yet no one can say he speaks falsely.
I am the father of this world,
saving those who suffer and are afflicted.
Because of the befuddlement of ordinary people,
though I live, I give out word I have entered
    extinction.
For if they see me constantly,
arrogance and selfishness arise in their minds.
Abandoning restraint, they give themselves up
    to the five desires
and fall into the evil paths of existence.
Always I am aware of which living beings
practice the way, and which do not,
and in response to their needs for salvation
I preach various doctrines for them.

At all times I think to myself:
How can I cause living beings
to gain entry into the unsurpassed way
and quickly acquire the body of a Buddha?
(*The Lotus Sutra and Its Opening and
Closing Sutras*, pp. 270–73)

Glossary

Buddha: "Enlightened One." One who correctly perceives the true nature of all phenomena and leads others to attain enlightenment. The nature of a Buddha exists in all beings and is characterized by the qualities of wisdom, courage, compassion, and life force.

"Expedient Means" chapter of the Lotus Sutra: The second of the twenty-eight chapters of the Lotus Sutra, in which Shakyamuni Buddha reveals that the purpose of a Buddha's advent in the world is to lead all people to enlightenment. Shakyamuni shows that all people have the potential for Buddhahood. This is the principal chapter of the theoretical teaching (the sutra's first half) and one of the two pivotal chapters of the entire sutra, the other being the "Life Span of the Thus Come One" (sixteenth) chapter, the core of the essential teaching (latter half).

Gohonzon: The object of devotion in Nichiren Buddhism. The embodiment of the Law of Nam-myoho-renge-kyo, expressing the life state of Buddhahood, which all people inherently possess. *Go* means worthy of honor, and *honzon* means an object of fundamental respect.

human revolution: An inner transformation by which people cultivate and come to express their highest human qualities, enabling them to change their circumstances as well. This process is a revolution in the character, in the life, of an individual human being.

kosen-rufu: Widespread propagation, or wide proclamation and dissemination. It is a term from the Lotus Sutra that literally means to declare and spread widely—Shakyamuni Buddha's injunction to his followers. The spread of the essence of the Lotus Sutra, Nam-myoho-renge-kyo, will bring about peace and happiness in the world. Therefore, kosen-rufu also refers to the creation of a peaceful, happy, and prosperous society based on the humanistic principles of Nichiren Buddhism.

"Life Span" chapter of the Lotus Sutra: The sixteenth chapter of the twenty-eight chapters of the Lotus Sutra, in which Shakyamuni Buddha reveals that he originally attained enlightenment in the far distant past rather than in his present life in India as his listeners generally thought. This chapter concludes with a verse section, which restates the important teachings of the preceding prose section. This is the principal chapter of the essential teaching (latter half) and one of the two pivotal chapters of the entire sutra, the other being the "Expedient Means" (second) chapter, the core of the theoretical teaching (first half).

Nam-myoho-renge-kyo: The name of the fundamental Law of life and the universe expounded in Nichiren Buddhism. The literal meaning is: *Nam* (devotion), the action of practicing Buddhism; *myoho* (Mystic Law), the essential law of life and its phenomenal manifestations; *renge* (lotus), the simultaneity of cause and effect; *kyo* (sutra), the truth expressed through the sound of one's voice.

Nichiren Daishonin (1222–82): The founder of the Buddhist teaching upon which the SGI bases its activities for peace and happiness in the world. He established the chanting of Nam-myoho-renge-kyo to the Gohonzon as the universal practice for attaining enlightenment. The name *Nichiren* means sun lotus, and *Daishonin* is an honorific title that means great sage.

Nikko Shonin (1246–1333): Nichiren Daishonin's designated successor. He concentrated on propagating his mentor's teachings, educating disciples, and collecting and transcribing his mentor's writings.

protective functions: Literally, heavenly beings and benevolent deities. Referred to also in Buddhist texts as heavenly gods and benevolent deities, Buddhist gods, protective gods, etc. These are inherent functions of nature and society that protect practitioners who uphold the correct Buddhist teaching. They function to protect the people and their land, and bring good fortune to both. These protective functions gain strength through one's Buddhist practice. They also indicate the protective or supportive actions of other people.

Shakyamuni: Also known as Gautama Buddha. The founder of Buddhism. *Shakyamuni* means "sage of the Shakyas," Shakya being the name of the tribe or clan to which his family belonged. The many Buddhist sutras are regarded as records of teachings expounded by Shakyamuni.

Soka Gakkai: Value Creation Society. The lay organization that promotes Nichiren Daishonin's teachings for peace and happiness. The Soka Gakkai was founded in 1930 in Japan, and the SGI, Soka Gakkai International, was established in 1975 on Guam.

three founding presidents: Tsunesaburo Makiguchi (1871–1944) was the first Soka Gakkai president. An educator and scholar, he developed the philosophy of value creation (*soka*), from which the Soka Gakkai gets its name. Together with Josei Toda (1900–58), he founded the Soka Gakkai in 1930 and taught that practicing Nichiren Daishonin's teaching is the means for leading a life of the highest values and greatest good. Both Mr. Makiguchi and Mr. Toda were imprisoned by the Japanese wartime government for their unyielding opposition to the militarist regime and its forced imposition of state-sponsored religion. Mr. Makiguchi died at age seventy-three during his incarceration. Mr. Toda became the second president in 1951. After World War II, he led the reconstruction of the Soka Gakkai, taking the membership from 3,000 to more than 750,000. Mr. Toda's closest disciple, Daisaku Ikeda (1928–), became the third president in

1960. He took office as the first SGI president in 1975. Under his leadership, Nichiren Buddhism has spread to nearly two hundred countries and territories. These three founding presidents, due to their committed efforts and dauntless spirit, are honored as the eternal mentors of kosen-rufu.

Three Great Secret Laws: The core principles of Nichiren Daishonin's teaching. They are the object of devotion of the essential teaching [the Gohonzon], the *daimoku* of the essential teaching [Nam-myoho-renge-kyo], and the sanctuary of the essential teaching [where we enshrine and chant to the Gohonzon]. Here, "essential teaching" refers to the teaching of Nam-myoho-renge-kyo and not to the essential teaching, or the latter fourteen chapters, of the Lotus Sutra. The Three Great Secret Laws represent Nichiren's embodiment of the Mystic Law, to which he was enlightened, in a form that all people can practice and thereby gain access to that Law within their own lives.